50 CREATIVE DATES FOR COUPLES

STAYING CONNECTED, ONE DATE AT A TIME

Written by

Razana Gober

50 CREATIVE DATES FOR COUPLES

STAYING CONNECTED, ONE DATE AT A TIME

Publisher: Paris Press
Author: Razana Gober
Illustrations: Owned by Razana Gober

Published in the United States of America.
ISBN: 978-1-966915-00-3

For permission requests, write to:

Email: razanaangel@yahoo.com, Instagram @razanagober LinkedIn: Razana Gober

Razana Gober asserts the moral right to be identified as the author of this work.

Designations used by companies to distinguish their products are often claimed as trademarks. All brand names and product names used in this book and on its cover are trade names, service marks, trademarks and registered trademarks of their respective owners. The publishers and the book are not associated with any product or vendor mentioned in this book. None of the companies referenced within the book have endorsed the book.

Disclaimer: This book is intended to provide helpful and informative material on the subjects addressed. It is not a substitute for professional advice. The author and publisher disclaim any liability arising from the use or application of the contents of this book.

To my husband, Ian,

Thank you for always encouraging new date ideas, keeping our relationship alive with endless fireworks. I love you!

Acknowledgments

To my father-in-law,

Thank you for treating me like your own daughter. We couldn't have accomplished this without your unwavering encouragement and support—it means the world to us. You are the best grandfather and an incredible father!

Table Of Contents

Introduction

Balancing Love and Parenting

Becoming a parent transforms your life in countless ways—sleepless nights, diaper changes, endless feedings, and a new human who depends on you for everything. It's exciting, overwhelming, and indescribably rewarding. But in the swirl of caring for a baby under two, it's easy for your relationship to slip into autopilot.

Why Dates Matter

Date nights (and days!) aren't just a luxury; they're vital for maintaining a healthy partnership. When you carve out time to focus on each other—whether for ten minutes or a whole evening—you're nurturing the core relationship that holds your family together.

How This Book Helps

This book offers <u>50 creative date ideas</u> suited for parents of young children. Some dates include your baby, others require a babysitter, and several can be done in 30 minutes or less. Mix and match based on your schedule, budget, and energy level. The key is to stay intentional—your relationship will thank you.

General Tips

1. Plan Around Nap Times: Choose a slot when your baby is typically well-rested or sleeping.

2. Babysitter Coordination: If going out, ensure you have clear instructions ready for whoever is caring for your baby.

3. Budget Friendly: Many of these ideas cost little or no money—love and creativity go a long way.

4. Stay Flexible: Babies are unpredictable. If a date doesn't go as planned, laugh it off and try another idea later.

Ready? Let's dive in!

Chapter One

At-Home Date Ideas

Introduction

Life with a baby under two can be hectic—sleepless nights, endless feedings, and unpredictable schedules can leave little room for romance. Yet finding moments to reconnect at home can help you maintain the spark in your relationship. The following at-home date ideas are designed to be flexible, fun, and mindful of a new parent's realities: limited time, occasional interruptions, and a need for low-stress planning.

01. Candlelight Dinner After Bedtime

Why This Works

Creates a romantic atmosphere without needing a babysitter, turning an ordinary evening into something special.

How to Plan

1. Choose the Night: Pick an evening when your baby's schedule is fairly predictable, so you can enjoy the meal uninterrupted.

2. Set the Scene: Dine at the table, on the patio, or even on a cozy living room floor picnic. Dim the lights and add candles or fairy lights for ambiance.

3. Dress the Part: Change into date-night attire. Cook (or order in) something a step above your usual fare.

Real-Life Scenario

Jenna and Luke wait until their baby's in deep sleep, then transform the living room into a romantic "restaurant." Their baby monitor is close by, but they dedicate this pocket of time solely to each other—complete with slow jazz playing softly.

Variations

Theme Night: Italian trattoria vibe with pasta and red wine, or a French bistro with baguettes and Edith Piaf in the background.

Outdoor Twist: If you have a safe, private outdoor space, try dining under the stars.

Optional Extras

Handwritten Menus: Make it feel like a true restaurant date by handwriting a menu or printing one out.

Shared Dessert: Whip up or purchase a fancy dessert like crème brûlée or chocolate lava cake.

Tips for Success

Interrupted by Baby: It's okay to pause and come back—reheat the meal in the oven if needed.

No Time to Cook: Order from your favorite restaurant, then plate it nicely.

Resource Recommendations

Music Streaming Services (Spotify, Apple Music) for "Romantic Dinner" playlists.

Meal Kit Services (HelloFresh, Blue Apron) to simplify cooking.

02. Home Spa Night

Why This Works

Encourages relaxation and closeness, helping both partners de-stress and feel pampered.

How to Plan

1. Create a Calm Environment: Dim lights, use scented candles or essential oil diffusers, and play soft music.

2. Choose Your Treatments: Face masks, foot soaks, massages, or a bubble bath if you have time.

3. Take Turns: One partner enjoys a treatment while the other provides it, then switch roles.

Real-Life Scenario

Carlos and Mei turn their living room into a mini spa once a month. They warm towels in the dryer, give each other gentle neck massages, and sip chamomile tea to end the night.

Variations

Pajama Party: Keep it casual and comfy with matching PJs.

Spa Tub Soak: If you have a bathtub and baby is asleep soundly, enjoy a candlelit soak together.

Optional Extras

DIY Scrubs: Mix sugar and coconut oil or oatmeal and honey for exfoliating scrubs.

Couple's Meditation: Close the evening with a short guided meditation to deepen relaxation.

Tips for Success

Limited Time: Even 20-minute foot soaks can feel indulgent if uninterrupted.

Baby Monitor: Keep it near so you won't stress about missing any cries.

Resource Recommendations

Calm / Headspace: Meditation apps with sleep stories, relaxing music, and guided sessions.

Pinterest: DIY spa recipes for face masks, bath bombs, and more.

03. Movie Night Upgrade

Why This Works

Turns a common activity (watching a movie) into an event that feels more date-like.

How to Plan

1. Set the Mood: Gather blankets and pillows, dim the lights, and perhaps build a fort in the living room for a fun twist.

2. Pick a Movie: Revisit a classic you both love or try something brand-new you've been curious about.

3. Upgrade the Snacks: Make specialty popcorn (cheddar, caramel, or chocolate) and pair with candy or homemade nachos.

Real-Life Scenario

Tina and Brandon host a "home film festival" once a month, selecting two indie shorts. They critique each afterward like film buffs, making the night feel more interactive.

Variations

Themed Night: Match the film's setting with your food and drinks (e.g., Japanese film + sushi and green tea).

Projector Feel: If possible, project the film on a blank wall for a mini-cinema atmosphere.

Optional Extras

Intermission Chat: Pause halfway to discuss the movie so far or guess what happens next.

Bonus Features: Watch behind-the-scenes clips or bloopers if available.

Tips for Success

Baby Interruptions: Pause guilt-free; the movie will wait.

Differing Tastes: Take turns choosing the genre or theme to keep it fair.

Resource Recommendations

Streaming Services: Netflix, Hulu, Disney+, Amazon Prime.

Watch Party Apps: Teleparty for remote viewing if one partner is traveling.

04. Board Game or Puzzle Night

Why This Works

Encourages conversation, teamwork, or friendly rivalry without screens—perfect for bonding.

How to Plan

1. Select Your Game: Choose quick card games or a puzzle you can handle on a coffee table.

2. Create a Fun Atmosphere: Play upbeat music, arrange snacks, and sit comfortably on cushions or chairs.

3. Friendly Stakes: Winner picks the next date's theme, or the loser does tomorrow's laundry—keep it playful.

Real-Life Scenario

Omar and Hazel enjoy cooperative games like Pandemic, working together while their baby occasionally babbles from the playpen.

Variations

Themed Games: Play a detective board game with suspenseful background music, or go retro with classic board games.

Progressive Puzzle: If time is limited, work on a larger puzzle over multiple nights.

Optional Extras

Snack Station: A small charcuterie board or treats within arm's reach.

Scoreboard: Track victories over time to see who's the reigning champ.

Tips for Success

Baby Involvement: If awake, let them watch or hold large, safe puzzle pieces (supervised).

Short on Time: Pick quick card games like UNO or Exploding Kittens.

Resource Recommendations

Two-Player Games: Jaipur, Patchwork, 7 Wonders Duel.

High-Quality Puzzles: Ravensburger, Buffalo Games.

05. Memory Lane

Why This Works

Nostalgia fosters closeness, letting you reflect on shared experiences and appreciate your history together.

How to Plan

1. Collect Memories: Gather photo albums, wedding videos, or digital slideshows.

2. Recreate a Special Moment: Cook a meal from your first date, listen to your wedding playlist, or reminisce about milestones.

3. Share Future Dreams: Talk about goals and aspirations for your relationship or your child's future.

Real-Life Scenario

Gina and Noah dig up their wedding slideshow each anniversary, laughing over awkward dance moves and finishing the night by writing new letters to each other for next year.

Variations

Memory Box: If you kept ticket stubs or postcards, revisit them and tell the stories behind each item.

Video Messages: Record a short video to your future selves—something to watch on a future anniversary.

Optional Extras

Scrapbooking: Glue photos, write captions, and decorate pages with stickers.

Playlist Throwback: Make a custom playlist of songs from your dating days.

Tips for Success

Emotional Moments: Embrace any nostalgia or tears—this is all part of deepening your bond.

Include Baby Briefly: Show them funny pictures or share short stories aloud, even if they can't understand yet.

Resource Recommendations

Photo Printing Sites: Shutterfly, Snapfish for physical albums.

Digital Frames: Set up a rotating slideshow of your favorite photos.

06. DIY Craft Night

Why This Works

Sparks creativity, collaboration, and fun while producing a tangible keepsake or piece of art.

How to Plan

1. Pick a Project: Painting, making candles, creating a vision board—choose something doable in an evening.

2. Set Up a Workspace: Cover surfaces with newspaper or a drop cloth. Lay out supplies beforehand for easy access.

3. Enjoy the Process: Don't worry about perfection. Laugh at paint splatters or crooked edges—focus on bonding.

Real-Life Scenario

Sam and Felicia painted abstract art on canvas. Despite no art experience, they had a blast and hung their creations in the living room.

Variations

Baby-Related Crafts: Personalize a onesie, craft a growth chart, or paint wooden letters of your baby's name.

Seasonal Decorations: DIY ornaments for the holidays or wreaths for different seasons.

Optional Extras

Craft Snacks: Finger foods like fruit skewers or cookies to keep you fueled.

Cocktails/Mocktails: Sip something tasty while you work to enhance the festive vibe.

Tips for Success

Mess Management: Pick projects you can pause quickly if the baby wakes.

Beginner-Friendly Kits: Stores or online shops often sell all-in-one craft kits.

Resource Recommendations

YouTube Tutorials: Find step-by-step videos for painting, candle-making, and more.

Pinterest: Inspiration boards for endless DIY ideas.

07. Book Club for Two

Why This Works

Encourages intellectual connection and deeper discussions beyond daily routines or baby talk.

How to Plan

1. Select a Book or Topic: Pick a short novel, non-fiction selection, or even a handful of interesting articles.

2. Read Separately: Use the week (or two) to read at your own pace.

3. Discuss in "Club" Format: Meet on date night, share insights, and reflect on the material together.

Real-Life Scenario

Chris and Anya rotate genres each month: one chooses a sci-fi novel, the other picks a personal development book. They look forward to "meeting night" with tea and quiet conversation.

Variations

Short Stories / Essays: Less pressure to finish a long book in limited time.

Article Swap: If a full book is too much, each partner picks an interesting piece to read and discuss.

Optional Extras

Theme Your Snacks: If reading a French novel, snack on croissants; a British mystery, sip on tea and biscuits.

Reading Aloud: Share a poignant paragraph or a poem by reading it to each other.

Tips for Success

Busy Schedules: Set realistic reading goals—no need to rush.

Different Interests: Alternate who chooses the material to expand both horizons.

Resource Recommendations

Libby / OverDrive: Borrow eBooks and audiobooks from your library.

Goodreads: Explore ratings, reviews, and track your reads.

08. Stargazing in Your Backyard

Why This Works

Offers a tranquil setting for meaningful conversation and a sense of wonder.

How to Plan

1. Pick the Right Night: Check a weather or astronomy app for clear skies. A new moon will give you darker skies for better viewing.

2. Set Up Comfortably: Spread blankets, prop up pillows, or use lawn chairs. Turn off indoor lights to reduce glare.

3. Spot the Stars: Use a stargazing app or a simple star chart to identify constellations.

Real-Life Scenario

Karen and Will love sipping hot cocoa while lying on a blanket under the stars. They share dreams about the future, occasionally spotting shooting stars (or passing planes!).

Variations

Telescope Fun: If you have a telescope, try finding planets or the moon's surface details.

Nighttime Sounds: Listen for crickets, owls, or even distant trains for a peaceful soundtrack.

Optional Extras

Soft Music: Play instrumental tunes gently in the background.

Written Wishes : Each writes down a wish or goal under the stars for later reflection.

Tips for Success

Light Pollution: If city lights are too bright, consider a nearby safe, open area like a local park.

Mosquitoes: Use baby-safe repellents or set up a mosquito net.

Resource Recommendations

SkyView / Star Chart Apps: Identify constellations and track planets in real-time.

Local Astronomy Clubs: Some host free star parties or provide tips for beginners.

Conclusion

At-home dates are a wonderful way to nurture your relationship without the stress of lining up childcare or traveling. By using the pockets of quiet time you have—especially after your baby is asleep—you can create meaningful, engaging experiences. Whether you opt for a romantic dinner, a spa-like retreat, or a simple puzzle night, the key is focusing on each other. Embrace the convenience and intimacy of staying in, and remember that even the occasional interruption by your little one can be part of the charm.

Chapter
Two

Baby-Friendly Outings

Introduction

Getting out of the house with a baby under two can feel like an Olympic sport—but it's also a chance to explore the world as a family and keep the spark alive in your relationship. In this chapter, you'll find date ideas that accommodate little ones without sidelining your need for couple time. From leisurely stroller walks to vibrant farmers' markets, these outings help you engage with each other while letting your baby safely tag along. With a bit of preparation (and a well-stocked diaper bag), you can savor the fresh air, *discover new local gems, and carve out fun moments—together.*

01. Stroller Walk in the Park

Why This Works

Fresh air, gentle exercise, and a chance to bond as a family while including the baby.

How to Plan

1. Pick a Scenic Spot : Choose a stroller-friendly park, nature trail, or waterfront walkway.

2. Pack the Essentials: Bring diapers, wipes, baby snacks (if age-appropriate), water for you, and a lightweight blanket for impromptu breaks.

3. Make It Special : Turn the walk into a mini date by holding hands, snapping selfies, or stopping for a quick stretch or coffee if there's a nearby café.

Real-Life Scenario

Rachel and Mike make Saturday mornings their "stroller stroll" time. They grab coffee on the way, walk along a lakeside trail, and stop halfway to feed ducks. It's become a weekly family ritual.

Variations

Photo Walk: Bring a camera or phone to capture interesting scenery or family moments.

Nature Bingo: Create a simple checklist (birds, squirrels, bridges) and see who spots them first.

Optional Extras

Playlist: Play a shared playlist or audiobook softly on your phone.

Picnic Stop: Bring a small picnic to enjoy mid-walk.

Tips for Success

Baby Gets Fussy: Go during a typical "happy" time (after a nap or feeding). Consider wearing your baby in a carrier if they dislike the stroller.

Weather Woes: Have a backup indoor spot in mind (like a large mall or community center) if it rains or gets too hot/cold.

Resource Recommendations

AllTrails App: Helps find local stroller-friendly trails.

Local Parks Department Website: Find park maps and event calendars.

02. Coffee Shop Break

Why This Works

Quick outing that combines a treat for parents (caffeine) and a calm environment to chat.

How to Plan

1. Find a Baby-Friendly Café: Look for one with spacious seating, outdoor patios, or high chairs.

2. Treat Yourselves: Order your favorite drinks and a snack to share; keep your baby engaged with a small toy or board book.

3. Enjoy Quality Time: Try talking about non-baby topics: hobbies, shows, or future travel ideas (even if it's just dreaming!).

Real-Life Scenario

Alex and Jess stop by a local café after every well-baby checkup. While baby dozes or people-watches, they savor their drinks and discuss weekend plans.

Variations

Drive-Thru & Park: If going inside is tough, grab coffee at a drive-thru and head to a scenic overlook or park.

Coffee Tasting at Home: Buy specialty beans at the café, then recreate a "coffee date" at home during naptime.

Optional Extras

Pastry Splurge: Indulge in a pastry you both love to make the moment sweeter.

Small Gift Exchange: Surprise each other with a tiny treat (like a cute mug or favorite cookie).

Tips for Success

Baby Restlessness: Take turns stepping outside with the baby if they need a change of scenery.

Time Constraints: Plan around a typical nap time or calmer part of the day for a smoother outing.

Resource Recommendations

Yelp / Google Maps: Search "family-friendly café" for reviews mentioning stroller access and kid-friendliness.

03. Storytime at the Library

Why This Works
Encourages early literacy and offers an entertaining, low-cost outing for parents and babies.

How to Plan
1. Check Schedules: Many libraries host free weekly baby/toddler story sessions.

2. Arrive Early: Grab a comfy spot and let your baby adjust to new sights and sounds.

3. Stay for Play: Some libraries have children's play areas or craft stations afterward.

Real-Life Scenario
Sarah and Brian attend a local library's "Baby & Me" storytime. They love the puppet shows, songs, and bubble-time that keep their little one mesmerized.

Variations
Book Exchange: Bring gently used children's books to donate or swap if the library allows.

Storytime at Home: If you can't make it in person, replicate the atmosphere at home by reading with silly voices or using puppets.

Optional Extras
Library Scavenger Hunt: After storytime, explore the kid's section looking for specific types of books (e.g., animal stories).

Meeting Other Parents: Use this chance to chat and swap tips with other caregivers.

Tips for Success

Overstimulation: Step out if baby gets fussy or overwhelmed, then come back in quietly.

Crowded Sessions: Sign up in advance if space is limited, or ask about less busy times.

Resource Recommendations

Library Website or App: Stay updated on storytimes, special events, and registration details.

Local Parenting Groups: Great for learning about library events or forming playdate connections.

04. Farmer's Market Adventure

Why This Works

Transforms a grocery run into a fun, sensory-rich family outing.

How to Plan

1. Choose the Right Time: Go early to avoid crowds and beat the midday heat.

2. Explore Together: Taste local produce, chat with vendors, and pick fresh ingredients for dinner.

3. Engage Your Baby: Let them explore the smells and colors—soft fruits (if old enough) can be safe for sampling.

Real-Life Scenario

Derek and Ana turned Saturday market trips into a foodie date. They each pick one new ingredient (like exotic cheese or a colorful veggie) to try in a home-cooked meal that evening.

Variations

Mini Picnics: Some markets have seating or live music—grab a quick bite on-site.

Farm-to-Table Dinner: Plan a recipe around a new or seasonal ingredient you both discovered.

Optional Extras

Reusable Bags & Carrier: Keep hands free and reduce waste by bringing your own bags.

Kids' Corner: Some markets have children's activities like face painting or music.

Tips for Success

Navigating Crowds: Opt for a baby carrier if the stroller is cumbersome in tight spaces.

Budget-Friendly: Set a spending limit; focus on fresh, seasonal produce for the best deals.

Resource Recommendations

Local Harvest: Find farmers' markets near you.

Pinterest: Endless recipe inspiration for seasonal produce.

05. Zoo or Aquarium Visit

Why This Works

Stimulates your baby's senses while providing fun, educational moments for the whole family.

How to Plan

1. Plan Your Route : Check the map beforehand; choose a few must-see exhibits to avoid overstimulation or endless walking.

2. Pack Wisely: Bring a stroller or carrier, sunscreen, extra clothes, and easy snacks.

3. Capture Memories: Take photos or videos of your baby's expressions as they watch fish or animals up close.

Real-Life Scenario

Mel and Chris visit their aquarium on weekday mornings to avoid crowds. They point out colorful fish and narrate the exhibits to engage their baby.

Variations

Membership Pass: If you love visiting, an annual pass often saves money.

Petting Zoo: For babies who can sit or stand, gentle interactions with small animals can spark curiosity.

Optional Extras

Guided Tour: Some zoos or aquariums offer short, child-friendly guided tours.

Souvenir: Pick out a small stuffed animal to remember the trip.

Tips for Success

Nap Overlaps: Go right after a nap so baby is fresh and alert.

Crowds: Avoid peak times (weekends or holiday breaks) if your baby is easily overwhelmed.

Resource Recommendations

Official Zoo/Aquarium Websites: Check for event calendars, parent-and-me programs, and discount days.

06. Outdoor Picnic

Why This Works

Combines nature, relaxation, and quality time in a casual, low-stress setting.

How to Plan

1. Choose a Spot : Parks, beaches, or your own backyard work well.

2. Keep It Simple: Finger foods like sandwiches, fruit, veggies, or cheese cubes are easy to prep and eat.

3. Add a Little Fun: Bring a ball, bubbles, or a storybook to keep your baby entertained and engage all of you.

Real-Life Scenario

Daniel and Priya do evening picnics once a month at a local park. Their baby crawls on the blanket while they share take-out and watch the sunset.

Variations

Sunset Picnic: Bring a small speaker for mellow background music as you watch the sky change colors.

Theme Picnic: Mexican night with tacos, salsa, and guac; or Italian with pasta salad and fresh mozzarella.

Optional Extras

Decorative Touches: String lights, lanterns, or a colorful blanket to elevate the vibe.

Outdoor Games: Frisbee or lawn games if your baby is content watching for a few minutes.

Tips for Success

Weather Changes: Keep an eye on the forecast; have an indoor backup plan.

Insect Issues: Bring baby-safe bug spray or citronella candles.

Resource Recommendations

Waterproof Picnic Blanket: Easy to clean and comfortable for the baby to sit or crawl on.

Portable High Chair: Handy if your baby is already eating solids.

07. Botanical Garden Stroll

Why This Works

Provides a peaceful, sensory-rich environment where babies can see vibrant colors and parents can enjoy tranquility.

How to Plan

1. Pick the Perfect Garden: Choose one known for stroller-accessible paths and scenic displays.

2. Go at a Calmer Time: Weekday mornings or late afternoons are typically less crowded.

3. Make It Educational : Read plant labels, use a plant ID app, or simply appreciate the variety of flora together.

Real-Life Scenario

Katie and Louis have a garden membership. They visit monthly to observe seasonal changes, snapping photos of their baby among blooming flowers.

Variations

Guided Tour: Participate in part of a guided walk if your baby's mood allows.

Artistic Inspiration: Bring a sketchbook or notebook for quick doodles or poetic musings.

Optional Extras

Picnic in the Garden: Some botanical gardens permit picnic areas— enjoy lunch with a view.

Flower Hunt: Make a mini game of finding flowers in every color of the rainbow.

Tips for Success

Allergies: Check pollen counts if anyone is sensitive.

Long Walks: Take plenty of breaks on benches to rest or feed the baby.

Resource Recommendations

Garden Websites: Look for free admission days or special seasonal exhibits.

Plant Identification Apps: E.g., PlantSnap or PictureThis.

08. Music in the Park

Why This Works

Outdoor concerts or music festivals are often free, relaxing, and family-friendly.

How to Plan

1. Find Local Events: Check community calendars for free concerts at parks or outdoor venues.

2. Pack the Essentials: Bring a blanket, snacks, weather-appropriate gear, and noise-cancelling headphones for the baby if it might get loud.

3. Relax & Enjoy: Sway to the music together, enjoy people-watching, or share a dance with your baby.

Real-Life Scenario

Tara and Jay look forward to summer jazz nights at their local park. They bring a blanket, a cooler of drinks, and dance with their baby to the slower tunes.

Variations

Evening Picnic & Show: Combine the concert with a sunset picnic—add flameless LED candles for ambiance.

Kids' Music Shows: Some events cater to children's songs and instruments, which can be extra engaging for babies.

Optional Extras

Glow Sticks: For evening events, they're safe, visually stimulating toys.

Dress Up: Turn it into a real "date" by wearing something a bit nicer than your usual parenting outfit.

Tips for Success

Noise Levels: If the music is amplified, use baby earmuffs or sit further from the speakers.

Crowds: Park near an exit for a quick getaway if baby becomes overwhelmed.

Resource Recommendations

Local City Websites: They often have "Concerts in the Park" or community festival listings.

Meetup / Facebook Events: Great resources for discovering smaller, family-friendly music gatherings.

Conclusion

Baby-friendly outings remind us that daily life doesn't have to be all routines and nap schedules—there's still plenty of room for adventure, even with a stroller in tow. Whether you're savoring a cup of coffee at a nearby café or exploring colorful market stalls, these simple dates bring back a sense of excitement and discovery to your relationship. Embrace the flexibility, enjoy the shared experiences, and watch your family bond deepen every step of the way.

Chapter Three

Quick Dates (30 Minutes or Less)

Introduction

Sometimes, all you have is a short window—maybe during a brief nap or after the baby finally drifts off. These bite-sized date ideas prove that meaningful connection doesn't have to consume your entire evening. A mere 10 to 30 minutes can be enough to recharge and remind each other you're more than just co-parents.

01. Sunrise Coffee Date

Why This Works

Early mornings can be peaceful if your baby is still asleep or quietly playing; watching a sunrise together sets a calm, romantic tone for the day.

How to Plan

1. Set an Alarm: Aim to wake 20-30 minutes before your baby's usual wake-up time.

2. Prep in Advance: Lay out mugs, coffee or tea supplies, and perhaps a small breakfast treat the night before.

3. Enjoy the View : Sit on your porch, balcony, or even by a window. Sip your beverages and watch the sky transition from night to day.

Real-Life Scenario

Maggie and Leo used to feel rushed every morning. Now, once a week, they set their alarms early for a quick coffee date. Even 15 minutes of tranquil conversation does wonders for their mood.

Variations

Outdoor Option: If you have a safe backyard, spread a blanket and enjoy the early birds chirping.

Light Stretch: Pair the sunrise with simple stretches or a few yoga poses.

Optional Extras

Breakfast Pastries: Grab croissants or muffins to make it feel more like a mini café experience.

Inspirational Reading: Share a short positive quote or daily devotional before starting your day.

Tips for Success

Baby Wakes Early: Bring them along in a bouncer or high chair. You can still enjoy the sunrise together as a trio.

Weather or Lack of View: If the sunrise isn't visible, just savor the quiet time indoors near a window.

Resource Recommendations

Sunrise Apps/Websites: Check exact sunrise times (e.g., TimeAndDate.com).

Low-Noise Coffee Makers: Single-serve or French press options to avoid waking the baby too soon.

02. Lunch Hour Meet-Up

Why This Works

Breaks up the workday and adds a spark of connection. Ideal if one or both parents work outside the home or have flexible midday schedules.

How to Plan

1. Coordinate Schedules: Pick a day when both can spare 30 minutes (or an hour if possible).

2. Simple Location: Meet at a nearby café, home, or even the parking lot at one partner's workplace.

3. Keep It Focused: Minimize distractions like phones or work talk—treat it like a mini date.

Real-Life Scenario

Sasha and Patrick both work from home but in separate rooms. Once a week, they schedule a shared lunch break—no laptops, just sandwiches and a short walk together.

Variations

Pack a Picnic: If the weather is nice, meet at a local park or outside seating area.

Quick Errand Date: Combine a necessary errand (like groceries) with a quick coffee or snack together.

Optional Extras

Bring a Surprise Treat: One partner could pick up a dessert or favorite drink for the other.

Conversation Starters: Ask a fun question (e.g., "What was the highlight of your week so far?").

Tips for Success

Strict Schedules: Communicate exact times to avoid stress or missing the window.

Baby Care: If baby is with a sitter or daycare, great; if not, bring them in a stroller or car seat for a "family lunch."

Resource Recommendations

Calendar Apps (Google Calendar, iCal) to schedule recurring lunch dates.

Meal Delivery (DoorDash, Uber Eats) if you're pressed for time.

03. Dessert-Only Date

Why This Works

Short, sweet, and satisfying. You don't need a full meal to enjoy a moment of indulgence together.

How to Plan

1. Pick a Dessert : Decide on a treat you both love (ice cream, pastries, or your favorite chocolate).

2. Serve It Up: If at home, plate it nicely. If going out, choose a local bakery or ice cream shop.

3. Focus on Fun: Chat about something light or dream up your next vacation—keep it sweet, just like the dessert.

Real-Life Scenario

Jon and Rita skip cooking an elaborate meal and instead share a fancy slice of cheesecake once the baby is asleep. They split it, savoring every bite at the kitchen island.

Variations

DIY Sundaes: At home, set up a toppings bar with sprinkles, sauces, and whipped cream.

Takeout Treat: Swing by a dessert food truck or a local bakery if you need fresh air.

Optional Extras

Presentation: Use fancy plates or stemware to elevate the experience.

Candlelight: Even if you're just splitting a brownie, candlelight adds instant romance.

Tips for Success

Late Night Cravings: If baby's bedtime is unpredictable, aim for a time they're usually down.

Avoid Overdoing Sugar: If you're sensitive to caffeine or sugar at night, pick a milder dessert.

Resource Recommendations

Dessert Recipe Sites: Allrecipes, Tasty for quick, easy sweets.

Local Bakery Guides: Yelp or Google for top-rated dessert spots nearby.

04. Power Walk

Why This Works

Combines a quick bit of exercise with bonding time. Perfect for clearing your head and boosting endorphins together.

How to Plan

1. Choose a Route : Around the block, a nearby park, or a safe neighborhood path.

2. Dress Comfortably: Slip on walking shoes and weather-appropriate clothes.

3. Engage in Conversation: Chat about your day, dreams, or simply enjoy the silence if you need a mental break.

Real-Life Scenario

Diana and Paul used to take turns watching the baby while the other exercised. Now, they do a 20-minute "couple's power walk" pushing the stroller. Even a short distance helps them reconnect.

Variations

Speed Walk Challenge: Try to maintain a brisk pace for an extra workout benefit.

Mini Jog: Alternate walking with brief intervals of slow jogging if you're both up for it.

Optional Extras

Music or Podcast: Listen together on speaker if you like, or share headphones (one earbud each).

Step Tracking: Use fitness apps or smartwatches to track your steps or pace.

Tips for Success

Baby on Board: If the baby is awake, use a stroller; if napping at home, ensure they're safe (with a monitor) and stay close by, or have someone else at home.

Time Constraints: Even a 10-minute loop is better than nothing—just get moving.

Resource Recommendations

Walking/Running Apps: MapMyWalk or Nike Run Club to log your route and stats.

Stroller-Friendly Communities: Look online for local maps or parent groups sharing safe walking spots.

05. Drive and Talk

Why This Works

Sometimes, a car ride is the only private time you get (especially if baby snoozes in the car seat). Changing scenery can spark fresh conversation.

How to Plan

1. Pick a Short Scenic Route: Maybe a loop around the neighborhood or a drive by a local waterfront.

2. Limit Distractions: Turn down the radio, stash phones, and focus on each other's company.

3. Talk Freely: Discuss topics you've been postponing or simply decompress about your day.

Real-Life Scenario

Helen and Marcus discovered that their fussy baby often calmed down in the car. They take a 20-minute scenic drive at dusk, allowing them to chat peacefully while baby nods off in the back seat.

Variations

Music Drive: If you both love music, create a short playlist of songs to share and discuss.

Morning Commute Chat: If you commute together, use part of that time to connect rather than just rushing in silence.

Optional Extras

Hot Beverage: Grab a coffee or hot cocoa in a travel mug to enjoy while you drive.

Scenery Stop: Park briefly to watch the sunset or city lights.

Tips for Success

Safety First: Don't let conversation distract from driving; use hands-free or pull over if needed.

Baby's Car Seat Comfort: Ensure the baby is secure and comfortable; a mirror to see them can help ease your mind.

Resource Recommendations

GPS Apps (Google Maps, Waze) for scenic routes or low-traffic times.

Conversation Starters: Apps like "Couple Game" or "Table Topics" can inspire deeper chats.

06. Mini Photo Shoot

Why This Works

Quick, creative, and leaves you with keepsakes of your journey as new parents.

How to Plan

1. Choose a Spot: Your backyard, living room, or a pretty corner of your home.

2. Set Up Your Phone/Camera: Use a self-timer or phone stand (a stack of books can work in a pinch).

3. Pose or Be Candid : Take silly shots, formal poses, or capture everyday moments like cooking together.

Real-Life Scenario

Ella and James do a 15-minute "family photo session" once a month. They snap a few couple shots and some with their baby to track everyone's growth and changing styles.

Variations

Theme It: Dress in matching colors, or pick a season or holiday theme.

Quick "Couple Selfies": If you're short on time, just snap a few selfies in a well-lit area.

Optional Extras

Props: Small chalkboard signs, fun hats, or a bouquet of flowers.

Music: Play an upbeat playlist to loosen up and capture natural smiles.

Tips for Success

Lighting: Natural daylight near a window often works best.

Baby Involvement: Include the baby in some shots if they're awake—get playful with them.

Resource Recommendations

Tripod / Phone Stand: Affordable options online.

Photo Apps: VSCO, Snapseed for quick editing or filters.

07. Meditation or Breathing Exercises Together

Why This Works

Offers a quick mental reset, grounding both partners and reducing stress.

How to Plan

1. Find a Quiet Spot: A corner of your living room, bedroom, or even the backyard if weather permits.

2. Select a Technique: Short guided meditation, box breathing, or a simple mindfulness practice.

3. Set a Timer: 5-10 minutes is enough to feel refreshed if you're consistent.

Real-Life Scenario

Rhea and Elliot commit to a 10-minute evening mindfulness session after putting their baby down. They report feeling calmer and more connected, even on hectic days.

Variations

Couple's Yoga: Add a few gentle poses or stretches if you have extra time.

Gratitude Practice: End by each sharing one thing you're grateful for that day.

Optional Extras

Soothing Music: Instrumental tunes or nature sounds as background.

Scented Candle: Lavender or chamomile scents can enhance relaxation.

Tips for Success

Interruptions: If baby wakes, attend to them and resume. A few short segments can still help.

No Pressure: Meditation is a practice—don't stress if thoughts wander.

Resource Recommendations

Meditation Apps: Headspace, Calm, Insight Timer.

YouTube Channels: "Yoga with Adriene," "Mindful Movement," etc.

08. Baby Nap Dance Party

Why This Works

Injects fun and energy into a brief window of free time—dancing is a mood booster and bonding activity.

How to Plan

1. Cue the Tunes: Create a short playlist of songs that get you moving and smiling.

2. Clear a Small Space: Living room, kitchen, or any area safe to dance.

3. Dance Like Nobody's Watching: Let loose, embrace silly moves, and enjoy each other's company without judgment.

Real-Life Scenario

Eve and Roland found they were too tired for a long workout but still wanted to stay active. They do a 15-minute "dance break" when their baby naps—laughter guaranteed!

Variations

Learn a Simple Routine: Check a quick YouTube dance tutorial if you want a structured dance.

Silent Disco: Each wears earbuds if you're worried about noise waking the baby.

Optional Extras

Video Record: Capture a snippet of your dance for fun memories or to see your progress if you try different routines.

Themed Music: 80s hits, Latin pop, or your wedding playlist—switch it up each time.

Tips for Success

Short on Time: Even 5 minutes can brighten your mood.

Worried About Noise: Keep volume moderate or do it in another room if the baby's nearby.

Resource Recommendations

Music Streaming Services: Curate a "Couple's Dance Mix."

Dance Tutorial Channels: e.g., "1 Million Dance Studio" or "The Fitness Marshall" for easy-to-follow moves.

Conclusion

Quick dates prove that deep connection doesn't always require a lengthy night out. Even 10-30 minutes can offer a much-needed pause to refocus on each other—whether that's dancing in the living room, grabbing a midday coffee together, or simply sharing a sweet treat. These micro-dates remind you that every moment counts and that love can thrive in small but meaningful doses.

Chapter Four

Babysitter-Required Adventures

Introduction

Sometimes, you need a date night (or day out) without the baby—no strollers, no nap schedule to juggle, just you two. While this may involve a bit more planning and securing childcare, it can offer a chance to reconnect on a deeper level and revisit the carefree vibe of your pre-baby days. Here are eight ideas that require a babysitter but reward you with valuable one-on-one time.

01. Dinner at Your Favorite Restaurant

Why This Works

Revisits an old favorite or lets you try a trendy spot, combining culinary delight with quality conversation.

How to Plan

1. Find a Trusted Babysitter: Ask friends, family, or use a reputable sitter service.

2. Pick the Restaurant: Make a reservation to avoid waiting. Choose somewhere special to make the most of your limited time.

3. Savor Each Course: Slow down. Order an appetizer or dessert you normally skip.

Real-Life Scenario

Haley and Jordan revisit the steakhouse where they first dined as a couple. They feel nostalgic, reminiscing about how far they've come since those early dates.

Variations

New Cuisine: Try a style of food you've never had before—Ethiopian, Thai, tapas, etc.

Chef's Tasting Menu: If you're foodies and have extra time and budget, indulge in a tasting menu for a memorable experience.

Optional Extras

Dress Up: Wear something that makes you feel confident—it's a date night, after all!

Cocktails/Mocktails: Start or end the meal with a special drink to toast the evening.

Tips for Success

Babysitter Prep: Leave clear instructions and contact info. Make sure the sitter knows bedtime routines if you'll be out late.

Time Constraints: If you only have a couple of hours, pick a restaurant close to home.

Resource Recommendations

Babysitter Platforms: Care.com, UrbanSitter, Sittercity.

Restaurant Apps: OpenTable or Resy for easy reservations.

02. Couples' Cooking Class

Why This Works

Hands-on, interactive experience that encourages teamwork and yields new kitchen skills to use later.

How to Plan

1. Search Local: OptionsLook for cooking schools, gourmet grocery stores, or community colleges offering evening classes.

2. Book in Advance: Popular classes fill up quickly—reserve your spots well ahead.

3. Have Fun: Embrace mistakes, learn new techniques, and laugh as you cook side by side.

Real-Life Scenario

Imani and Russell booked a sushi-making class. Although their rolls looked lopsided at first, they loved bonding over new skills—and now make sushi at home regularly.

Variations

Online Cooking Class: If you can't find a sitter for long, have them watch the baby in another part of the house while you follow a virtual class in the kitchen.

Private Chef Experience: Some local chefs offer private lessons for an intimate, personalized experience.

Optional Extras

Themed Outfit: Matching aprons or funny chef hats for playful photos.

Recipe Cards: Bring them home for future date-night dinners.

Tips for Success

Allergies/Dietary Needs: Confirm with the class host if you have restrictions.

Timing: Aim for a class that lasts no more than 2-3 hours if your baby is very young.

Resource Recommendations

Local Cooking Schools: Many offer date-night specials or couples' classes.

Cozymeal / Airbnb Experiences: Platforms that list unique cooking events in various cities.

03. Theater or Live Show

Why This Works

Provides entertainment outside your usual routine. Watching a performance can spark fun discussions afterward.

How to Plan

1. Pick a Show: Musicals, plays, comedy clubs, or even a local band—choose something you'll both enjoy.

2. Buy Tickets Early: Good seats often sell fast; planning ahead ensures a stress-free night.

3. Arrive with Time to Spare: Grab a drink or snack before the show starts, and settle in without rushing.

Real-Life Scenario

Tracy and Geoff score tickets to a local theater production of a famous musical. They spend intermission excitedly discussing the staging and songs, feeling invigorated by the cultural experience.

Variations

Outdoor Concert: If the weather's nice, find a local open-air venue for a relaxed vibe.

Improv Night: Comedy clubs or improv theaters can offer a lighthearted break from parenting stress.

Optional Extras

Pre/Post-Show Dessert: Make the outing feel longer with a sweet treat or coffee after the curtain call.

Dress Code: Dressing up for the theater can add to the sense of occasion.

Tips for Success

Babysitter Communication: Provide a show schedule so they know when you'll be unreachable or in silent mode.

Budget Options: Look for off-peak nights, matinees, or community theater tickets.

Resource Recommendations

Ticket Apps/Sites: Ticketmaster, TodayTix, or Goldstar for discounted or last-minute seats.

Local Arts Calendars: City websites or social media often list smaller productions.

04. Escape Room Challenge

Why This Works

Fun, immersive experience that requires teamwork, problem-solving, and communication—great for couples who love puzzles.

How to Plan

1. Find a Theme You Both Like: Mystery, sci-fi, heist, or horror—pick an escape room that piques your interest.

2. Invite Friends or Go Duo : Some rooms allow just two players; others may group you with strangers. Choose what suits you best.

3. Embrace the Challenge: Work collaboratively. Don't stress if you don't escape in time—enjoy the adrenaline rush.

Real-Life Scenario

Nadia and Greg book a "treasure hunt" escape room. They laugh over missed clues and celebrate small victories each time they unlock a puzzle, feeling closer by the end.

Variations

At-Home Escape Games: If babysitting time is tight, you could do a shorter puzzle box or "exit game" at home once the baby's asleep.

Haunted Themes: Around Halloween, many escape rooms have spooky twists for extra thrills.

Optional Extras

Friendly Competition: Compare your completion time to that of other teams.

Costume Night: Some rooms encourage dressing up in theme (e.g., detective hats for a noir-themed puzzle).

Tips for Success

Babysitter Timing: Escape rooms typically last 60 minutes plus check-in, so plan for about 90 minutes total.

Coordinate with Other Parents: If you join friends, you could share a babysitter or rotate nights off.

Resource Recommendations

Escape Room Directories: Sites like Escape Room Hub or EscapeRoomsNearMe.

Board Game Versions: EXIT: The Game, Unlock!, or Escape Room in a Box for at-home alternatives.

05. Bowling or Mini Golf

Why This Works

Lighthearted, casual, and reminiscent of classic date nights. Physical activities like these can spark playful competition.

How to Plan

1. Find a Local Venue: Bowling alleys or mini-golf courses are often open late; confirm hours in advance.

2. Invite Spontaneity: Don't worry about your score; focus on laughing, cheering each other on, and enjoying the carefree vibe.

3. Reward Yourselves: Grab a snack or beverage at the venue if time permits.

Real-Life Scenario

Alisha and Don revisit the bowling alley they loved in high school. They compete for fun "couple wagers," like who picks the next movie or date location.

Variations

Neon/Glow Bowling: Some alleys have special "cosmic bowling" nights with black lights and music.

Indoor Mini-Golf: If the weather is poor, look for indoor courses with creative themes.

Optional Extras

Silly Wagers: Loser does a chore of winner's choice, or winner picks dessert on the way home.

Themed Outfits: Coordinate colors or wear matching silly socks.

Tips for Success

Babysitter Hourly Limit: Keep an eye on time if your sitter has constraints.

Weekend Crowds: Go on a weekday evening if possible to avoid long wait times.

Resource Recommendations

Local Entertainment Guides: Find new, themed mini-golf spots or upgraded bowling alleys.

Group Deals: Groupon often has discounts for bowling or mini-golf packages.

06. Staycation Night

Why This Works

A mini getaway without traveling far. Enjoy hotel amenities and a change of scenery, even if it's in your own city.

How to Plan

1. Book a Room: Choose a local hotel or boutique inn. Look for features like a spa, pool, or room service to enhance relaxation.

2. Pack Light: One overnight bag with comfy clothes, maybe a swimsuit if there's a pool/hot tub.

3. Disconnect from Routine: Pretend you're on vacation—order room service, watch movies, and relish uninterrupted conversation.

Real-Life Scenario

Eric and Tasha live 20 minutes from a downtown hotel. They book a stay once every few months, leaving their baby with grandparents overnight. It feels like a luxurious escape from daily stress.

Variations

Daytime "Staycation": If you can't do overnight, book a hotel spa day pass or pool pass for a few hours.

Local B&B: Cozy bed-and-breakfasts can feel even more intimate.

Optional Extras

Romantic Touches: Champagne, rose petals, or a special dessert delivered to the room.

Tourist in Your City: Visit a local museum or landmark as if you're out-of-towners.

Tips for Success

Babysitter/Family Coordination: Ensure overnight care is well-prepared (clothes, formula/breastmilk, emergency numbers).

Budget: Look for midweek rates or last-minute hotel apps for deals if cost is a concern.

Resource Recommendations

Hotel Booking Apps: HotelTonight, Booking.com, or Airbnb for staycation options.

Local Guides: Sometimes city tourism sites list romantic package deals.

07. Museum Date

Why This Works

Stimulates conversation and curiosity, giving you a cultured, educational break from diapers and feeding schedules.

How to Plan

1. Pick Your Museum Type: Art, science, history, or a specialty museum that piques your interest.

2. Plan Your Route: Large museums can be overwhelming. Choose a couple of sections to explore fully.

3. Discuss and Observe: Pause to share opinions on exhibits, spark conversation, and learn from each other.

Real-Life Scenario

Andrea and Colin spend a Sunday afternoon at a modern art museum. They love analyzing each piece, joking about what they see, and occasionally learning new facts from the plaques.

Variations

Audio Guides: Grab headsets for deeper insights, then chat about the highlights.

Temporary Exhibits: Seek out special exhibits or traveling shows that interest you both.

Optional Extras

Café Break: Museums often have charming cafés—take a break for coffee or a quick bite.

Souvenir: A small magnet or postcard from the gift shop can be a fun memento.

Tips for Success

Babysitter Timing: Museums often take at least 2 hours to explore—plan accordingly.

Crowded Days: If possible, visit on weekdays or off-peak hours to avoid weekend crowds.

Resource Recommendations

Museum Websites: Check special events or discount/free admission days.

Local Cultural Listings: Newspaper or city guide apps often highlight new or notable exhibits.

08. Dance Class

Why This Works

⁻ Physical closeness, shared laughter, and learning new steps together can reignite sparks.

How to Plan

1. Choose a Style: Salsa, swing, ballroom, hip-hop—pick something you're both open to trying.

2. Find a Class: Look for couples' beginner sessions or dance studios that offer drop-in classes.

3. Go with the Flow : Don't worry about missteps. Have fun, laugh at mistakes, and support each other.

Real-Life Scenario

Mei and Victor sign up for a weekly salsa class. Though they step on each other's toes at first, they bond over practicing moves at home, turning house chores into mini dance sessions.

Variations

Online Tutorials: If babysitter availability is limited, do a virtual dance lesson after bedtime.

Wedding Dance Refresh: Relearn or update your wedding dance for a fun nostalgia trip.

Optional Extras

Dance Shoes: Proper footwear can make dancing more comfortable—especially for styles like ballroom or swing.

Dress Up: Wear outfits that let you move but also make you feel confident.

Tips for Success

Scheduling: Most group classes last around 60-90 minutes—perfect for an evening out.

Confidence: Don't be shy; everyone's learning. Embrace the fun vibe.

Resource Recommendations

Local Dance Studios: Check websites or social media for class schedules.

YouTube Channels: "Salsa Tutorial," "Shawn Trautman Dance," etc., for at-home practice.

Conclusion

Babysitter-required adventures can feel like a luxury for new parents, but carving out this kind of time is essential for rekindling intimacy and having grown-up fun. Whether it's savoring a favorite restaurant meal or learning a new dance step, these experiences help you remember who you are as a couple—beyond just being "Mom" or "Dad." With a reliable sitter and thoughtful planning, you can enjoy moments of carefree connection that refresh your relationship.

Chapter Five

Active & Outdoor Dates

Introduction

If you're an outdoorsy couple or just looking to get some exercise and sunshine, these active date ideas can bring fresh air into your routine. Many are baby-friendly, but we'll highlight ways to make them strictly for the two of you if needed. Embrace nature, movement, and the simple joy of being outside together.

01. Hiking with Baby

Why This Works

Provides gentle exercise, scenic views, and a chance to introduce your little one to nature.

How to Plan

1. Choose an Easy Trail: Look for flat or moderately inclined paths, ideally with shade.

2. Gear Up: A baby carrier or sturdy stroller designed for trails if it's not too rough.

3. Pace Yourselves: Take breaks for water, feeding, or just to enjoy the view.

Real-Life Scenario

Kristen and Dave started with a local one-mile nature loop. Their baby dozes in the carrier while they chat and point out birds and trees along the way.

Variations

Partner Hike: If you get a sitter, tackle a more challenging trail just for the two of you.

Nature Scavenger Hunt: Spot different types of leaves or wildlife sounds.

Optional Extras

Picnic Break: Bring simple snacks or lunch to enjoy at a scenic overlook.

Nature Photography: Snap photos of each other and interesting sights.

Tips for Success

Weather: Check the forecast; avoid extreme heat or cold.

Baby Comfort: Ensure sun protection, appropriate clothing, and keep an eye on their temperature.

Resource Recommendations

All Trails App: Filter hikes by difficulty and stroller-friendly routes.

Local Parks and Recreation: Websites often list easy nature walks.

02. Beach Day

Why This Works

Sun, sand, and water offer sensory experiences for both you and your baby (if they come along) or a relaxing vibe if you go as a couple alone.

How to Plan

1. Pick a Baby-Friendly Beach: One with gentle waves, lifeguards, and nearby facilities like restrooms.

2. Pack Essentials: Sunscreen, towels, umbrellas, extra clothes, and snacks.

3. Plan Activities: A quick dip, building sandcastles (if baby is older), or simply lounging with a good book.

Real-Life Scenario

Ava and Luke take their 1-year-old to a calmer lake beach. Baby splashes in the shallow water while they relax on a blanket, taking turns wading in deeper areas.

Variations

Sunset Stroll: Leave baby with a sitter and walk barefoot along the shoreline at dusk.

Water Sports: If you're adventurous and baby-free, try paddleboarding or kayaking.

Optional Extras

Portable Beach Tent: For shade and a safe spot for the baby to nap.

Seashell Hunt: Collect shells or pretty stones as a keepsake.

Tips for Success

Safety First: Keep baby within arm's reach near water; apply sunscreen often.

Crowd Control: Visit during off-peak times for a quieter experience.

Resource Recommendations

Beach Gear: Baby-safe floats, pop-up tents, and protective swimwear.

Local Beach Guides: Check water quality and safety advisories.

03. Biking Together

Why This Works

Low-impact cardio that can be adapted for baby-wearing (in a bike trailer or child seat) or as a couple's escape.

How to Plan

1. Check Your Bikes: Ensure tires are inflated and brakes work. If using a baby seat or trailer, follow weight limits and safety guidelines.

2. Pick a Safe Path: Preferably a dedicated bike lane, park trail, or quiet neighborhood roads.

3. Enjoy the Ride: Go at a leisurely pace, chat, or take in scenery.

Real-Life Scenario

Maia and Elijah attach a bike trailer for their toddler and explore a flat riverside trail every Sunday. They stop occasionally for snacks and photo ops.

Variations

Date Ride: If someone can watch the baby, pedal a longer scenic route or join a local bike tour.

E-Bikes: If you want less exertion, try electric bikes to cover more ground easily.

Optional Extras

Picnic Stop: Bring a backpack with sandwiches, fruit, and drinks.

Couple's Matching Helmets: A fun way to show your unity (safety first!).

Tips for Success

Helmet Fit: Make sure both adults and the baby have properly fitted helmets (if baby is old enough to sit in a trailer).

Weather Watch: Avoid extreme heat or rain; wind can be challenging for babies.

Resource Recommendations

Local Bike Share Programs: If you don't own bikes, many cities offer rentals.

Child Bike Trailers: Brands like Burley or Thule for high safety ratings.

04. Community Park Workout

Why This Works

Fitness and bonding in the fresh air, with options to include your baby or go solo as a couple.

How to Plan

1. Find a Park with Amenities: Look for one with a playground (if baby is old enough to enjoy it), open grassy fields, or outdoor exercise stations.

2. Create a Mini Routine: Warm-up walk, bodyweight exercises (squats, lunges), maybe some light jogging.

3. Tag-Team if Baby is Present: One parent watches baby while the other does a set, then switch.

Real-Life Scenario

Roland and Dana push their stroller to a local park. They alternate doing quick circuits of push-ups and squats around a picnic table while the other plays peek-a-boo with their little one.

Variations

Couple's Bootcamp: Attend a local group fitness class in the park if babysitting is available.

Yoga Session: Roll out mats in a quiet area for a quick yoga flow.

Optional Extras

Resistance Bands: Lightweight, easy to carry, and add variety to your workout.

Post-Workout Snack: Refuel with smoothies or protein bars.

Tips for Success

Short Sessions: A 20-minute workout is enough to break a sweat and bond.

Baby Breaks: If the little one gets fussy, adapt on the fly or incorporate them into gentle exercises (e.g., stroller lunges).

Resource Recommendations

Fitness Apps: Nike Training Club, FitOn for quick bodyweight workouts.

Local Meetups: "Stroller Strides" or parent-and-baby fitness groups.

05. Gardening Project

Why This Works

Combines the outdoors with a shared, productive hobby. You'll nurture something together—beyond just your baby!

How to Plan

1. Choose Your Plants: Herbs, flowers, or easy veggies. Consider your climate and sunlight availability.

2. Get Supplies: Pots, soil, gloves, a watering can. If you have a yard, prep a small garden bed.

3. Work as a Team: One digs holes or arranges seeds while the other handles watering or removing weeds.

Real-Life Scenario

Paula and Ben have a small patio. They plant herbs like basil, mint, and rosemary in pots, enjoying fresh additions to their cooking and a sense of teamwork.

Variations

Urban Gardening: Use windowsill boxes or vertical planters if you're in an apartment.

Flower Garden: Grow a cutting garden to have fresh flowers on the table.

Optional Extras

Decorative Touches: Paint pots or add garden ornaments.

Mini Gardening Date: If baby's awake, let them explore safe sensory experiences like touching soft leaves (supervised).

Tips for Success

Mess Factor: Dress in clothes you don't mind getting dirty; have a towel for quick cleanups.

Seasonal Adaptations: Choose plants that thrive in your current season or consider an indoor herb kit in winter.

Resource Recommendations

Gardening Apps: Blossom or Planter to track watering schedules and sunlight needs.

Local Nurseries: Often provide free advice on plants suitable for beginners.

06. Fishing or Kayaking

Why This Works

Peaceful water-based activities can be relaxing yet engaging. Good for couples who enjoy nature and a slower pace.

How to Plan

1. Pick the Right Spot: A local lake, river, or calm bay. Check regulations and whether you need permits.

2. Gear Check: Fishing rods, tackle box, or kayak rentals/personal kayaks with life jackets.

3. Enjoy the Silence: Part of the appeal is the soothing lull of water. Bring snacks, water, and a sense of adventure.

Real-Life Scenario

Jonah and Karina rent a tandem kayak at a nearby lake for an hour. They paddle leisurely, taking breaks to chat and enjoy the scenery— baby-free courtesy of Grandma.

Variations

Baby Along: If you have a calm toddler and proper safety gear, a short, stable boat ride can be an option.

Fly-Fishing Lessons: Turn it into a learning experience if you're both novices.

Optional Extras

Picnic on Shore: Pack a small cooler to enjoy after you dock.

Sunset Paddle: Evening kayaking can be magical—check safety guidelines for low light.

Tips for Success

Weather Check: Wind or storms can make water activities unsafe.

Safety First: Life jackets are a must, and follow local regulations.

Resource Recommendations

Local Outfitters: Some lakes or parks offer guided kayak tours or fishing lessons.

State Wildlife Agencies: Info on fishing permits and location guidelines.

07. Seasonal Activities

Why This Works

Embraces the best of each season, from apple picking in autumn to sledding in winter, providing variety throughout the year.

How to Plan

1. Check Local Farms or Seasonal Events: Apple orchards, pumpkin patches, sunflower fields, or Christmas tree farms.

2. Time It Right: Mornings often have fewer crowds; weekends can be busy but more festive.

3. Dress Appropriately: Comfortable, weather-appropriate clothing and shoes.

Real-Life Scenario

Michelle and Ted make a tradition of going apple picking each fall. They bring home fresh apples to bake pies, turning the harvest into another mini date at home.

Variations

Winter: Building a snowman, ice skating, or a short ski lesson if you have childcare.

Spring/Summer: Berry picking, lavender farms, or flower festivals.

Optional Extras

Photography: Seasonal backdrops can be stunning—capture new family or couple photos.

Themed Treats: Post-activity apple cider, hot chocolate, or fresh lemonade.

Tips for Success

Crowded Events: Aim for non-peak hours if your baby doesn't handle crowds well.

Allergies: Check pollen or outdoor allergen levels before going.

Resource Recommendations

Local Farm Directories: Websites like PickYourOwn.org list seasonal farms.

Community Event Calendars: Town websites often highlight festivals or seasonal celebrations.

08. Outdoor Movie Night

Why This Works

Combines fresh air with a cozy movie experience—perfect for warm, clear evenings.

How to Plan

1. Find or Create a Setup: If there's a local outdoor movie screening, great! If not, set up a projector in your backyard or driveway.

2. Bring Comfort Items: Blankets, lawn chairs, pillows, and maybe a mosquito-repellent lantern.

3. Snacks Galore: Popcorn, candy, or s'mores if you have a fire pit.

Real-Life Scenario

Serena and Kyle invite another couple over after their kids are asleep to watch a classic film projected on a garage wall. They chat softly and enjoy the starry sky overhead.

Variations

Drive-In Theater: If one is still operating near you, it can be a nostalgic experience.

Theme Night: Horror movie under the moonlight, or a rom-com with fairy lights.

Optional Extras

Ambient Lighting: String lights or tiki torches to set the mood.

Dress Code: Snuggly pajamas or comfy hoodies for cooler nights.

Tips for Success

Quiet Hours: Check local noise ordinances and be mindful of sleeping babies or neighbors.

Weather-Dependent: Have a backup plan if rain or wind rolls in.

Resource Recommendations

Portable Projectors: Affordable LED models work well for backyard setups.

Outdoor Screens: Or just use a white sheet hung tightly on a wall.

Conclusion

Spending time outdoors or staying active can revitalize your relationship—fresh air and shared movement do wonders for stress relief and reconnection. Whether you're hiking with the baby or kayaking for a child-free adventure, these active date ideas remind you that parenthood doesn't have to mean giving up on the fun of exploring the great outdoors together.

Chapter Six

Budget-Friendly Dates

Introduction

Diapers, formula, childcare expenses—it's no secret that parenting can strain a budget. But meaningful connection doesn't have to drain your wallet. These dates emphasize creativity and resourcefulness, proving that quality time is about presence, not price tags.

01. Window Shopping Date

Why This Works

A leisurely stroll browsing shops can be entertaining and spark conversation, without the pressure to buy anything.

How to Plan

1. Pick a Location: A local mall, downtown area, or cute shopping district.

2. Set a "No Buying" Rule: Unless you agree on a tiny treat, focus on looking, not purchasing.

3. Make It Fun: Comment on interesting items, guess prices, or imagine future purchases (like home décor ideas).

Real-Life Scenario

Karen and Thomas walk through a historical downtown area, peeking into antique stores. They get décor ideas and occasionally splurge on a $5 antique spoon as a keepsake.

Variations

Thrift Store Tour: Hunt for hidden gems or funny finds at secondhand shops.

Holiday Window Displays: Perfect around Christmas or other festive seasons.

Optional Extras

Coffee-to-Go: Enjoy a small coffee or treat as you wander.

Scavenger Hunt: Each tries to spot a unique themed item, like the ugliest vase or the coolest vintage record.

Tips for Success

Baby On Board: A stroller-friendly mall is perfect for bad weather days.

Budget: If you decide to buy something, set a low limit (e.g., under $10).

Resource Recommendations

Local Downtown Guides: Some towns have "First Friday" or "Art Walk" events.

Thrift Shop Directories: Yelp or Google for reviews on the best spots.

02. DIY Pizza Night

Why This Works

Cooking together can be fun and cost-effective. Personalizing pizzas ensures everyone gets their favorite toppings.

How to Plan

1. Gather Ingredients: Pre-made dough or a simple homemade dough recipe, sauce, cheese, veggies, meats, etc.

2. Assemble Together: Each person can craft their own mini pizza, or collaborate on one large pie.

3. Bake & Enjoy: Pop it in the oven, set a timer, and maybe dance in the kitchen while it cooks.

Real-Life Scenario

Wayne and Tara love making heart-shaped pizzas every Friday night. Even their toddler gets a mini dough piece to "decorate."

Variations

Grilled Pizza: If you have a grill, try crisping the dough outdoors for a smoky flavor.

Calzone or Flatbread: Switch up the style but keep the same concept.

Optional Extras

Topping Bar: Lay out bowls of peppers, onions, olives, pepperoni, mushrooms—whatever you like.

Theme Night: Italian music in the background, checkered tablecloth, and candles for a "pizzeria" feel.

Tips for Success

Baby Interruption: Prep ingredients ahead of time or use pre-chopped veggies so you can pause easily.

Diet-Friendly: Opt for whole-wheat dough, vegan cheese, or gluten-free crust if needed.

Resource Recommendations

Recipe Sites: Allrecipes or Food Network for easy pizza dough instructions.

Budget Grocery Apps: Look for deals on toppings or store-brand cheeses.

03. Community Events

Why This Works

Many local concerts, fairs, or festivals are free or low-cost, providing a fun outing for you and possibly your baby, too.

How to Plan

1. Check Local Listings: City websites, Facebook events, or community bulletin boards often list free weekend happenings.

2. Choose Something You Both Like: Live music, art fairs, cultural festivals—whatever sparks shared interest.

3. Go with the Flow: Arrive early to find good parking or seats. Wander at your own pace.

Real-Life Scenario

Steph and Damon discovered a free outdoor jazz concert series in their town. They bring a blanket, small cooler, and enjoy live music while their baby bounces along to the rhythm.

Variations

Farm-to-Table Festivals: Often feature local produce tasting, live demos, and kids' activities.

Library or Town Hall: Lectures, movie nights, or craft fairs can be surprisingly fun.

Optional Extras

Themed Outfits: Dress to match the event (e.g., folk festival in boho attire).

Picnic Pack: Snacks and drinks from home to avoid pricey vendor food.

Tips for Success

Crowd Size: If your baby is sensitive to noise or crowds, aim for smaller community events.

Backup Plan: If baby gets fussy, stroll around or find a quiet spot.

Resource Recommendations

City Websites: Official municipal sites often have event calendars.

Local News & Facebook Groups: Great sources for hidden-gem happenings.

04. Volunteer Together

Why This Works

Helping others can be deeply rewarding and a powerful way to bond through shared compassion.

How to Plan

1. Choose a Cause: Food banks, animal shelters, community clean-ups—something you both value.

2. Coordinate with Organizers: Find opportunities that either allow a baby on-site or arrange a babysitter if needed.

3. Contribute Your Skills: Cooking, sorting donations, cleaning—whatever feels meaningful.

Real-Life Scenario

Dan and Sylvia volunteer monthly at a community soup kitchen. Their baby stays with a grandparent for a couple of hours, and they return feeling fulfilled and closer.

Variations

Baby-Inclusive: Some donation drives or outdoor clean-ups might be okay with a stroller.

Remote Volunteering: If in-person isn't feasible, consider online volunteer tasks or making care packages at home.

Optional Extras

Invite Friends: Make it a group activity, fostering a sense of community.

Celebrate After: Grab coffee or a treat to talk about the experience.

Tips for Success

Scheduling: Many volunteer ops happen on weekends—sign up early if slots are limited.

Small Commitments: Even an hour can help if you're juggling baby duties.

Resource Recommendations

VolunteerMatch.org: Helps find local or virtual volunteer opportunities.

Local Nonprofits: Reach out directly to organizations you admire.

05. YouTube Dance Tutorials

Why This Works

Free, fun, and easy to pause if your baby needs attention. Dancing also boosts endorphins and fosters closeness.

How to Plan

1. Select a Style: Hip-hop, salsa, line dancing—whatever excites you both.

2. Clear Some Space: Make sure you can move safely without tripping over toys.

3. Follow Along; Laugh at mistakes; celebrate small progress.

Real-Life Scenario

Max and Lindsay have a nightly 15-minute dance practice after putting their baby to bed. They follow a K-pop dance tutorial, cracking up when they struggle with the moves—but loving the shared activity.

Variations

TikTok Challenges: Learn a short choreographed routine for quick gratification.

Couple's Routine: Try a partner dance tutorial (e.g., beginner salsa).

Optional Extras

Costume Fun: Wear matching workout gear or something silly to lighten the mood.

Record Yourself: For laughs later or to see improvement over time.

Tips for Success

Baby Monitor Ready: If you need to stop, no worries—just pick up where you left off.

Low-Impact Options: If you're postpartum, choose gentle dances.

Resource Recommendations

YouTube Channels: "The Fitness Marshall," "Mandy Jiroux," "Learn to Dance" for free lessons.

Bluetooth Speakers: Enhance audio and free up your phone screen for visuals.

06. Indoor Picnic

Why This Works

Weather-proof, cost-effective, and surprisingly romantic. Transform your living room into a cozy getaway.

How to Plan

1. Gather Picnic Supplies: A blanket, pillows, simple homemade snacks (sandwiches, fruit, cheese).

2. Create Ambiance: Dim lights, light candles (safely), or play soft music.

3. Relax & Chat: Eat on the floor together, focusing on conversation rather than screens.

Real-Life Scenario

Henry and Zoe live in a rainy city. They lay out a checkered blanket on the living room floor, nibble on crackers and cheese, and share funny stories from the week.

Variations

Theme It: Italian-style with bruschetta and sparkling water, or Spanish tapas if you're feeling fancy.

Storytelling: Each shares a travel story or future dream trip to keep the wanderlust alive.

Optional Extras

Mocktails: Whip up non-alcoholic drinks with fruit juices, garnishes, and a salt/sugar rim.

Board Games: Combine with a short card game or puzzle after the meal.

Tips for Success

Baby Factor: If the baby is awake, place them nearby on a safe mat with toys.

Easy Cleanup: Use a tray or hamper near you to toss used plates or utensils quickly.

Resource Recommendations

Pinterest: Great for indoor picnic aesthetic ideas.

Simple Recipe Sites: Skinnytaste, Budget Bytes for easy snack recipes.

07. Free Museum Days

Why This Works

Many museums offer free or discounted admissions on certain days/times, letting you soak up culture without extra cost.

How to Plan

1. Research Schedules: Search for "free museum days" in your city to find weekly or monthly deals.

2. Arrive Early: Free days can be busier, so go off-peak if possible.

3. Explore Select Exhibits: Large museums can be overwhelming—focus on a few sections you both find intriguing.

Real-Life Scenario

Gary and Alicia discovered that their local art museum has free admission every Wednesday after 3 PM. They plan an early dinner afterward, making it an artsy yet low-cost date.

Variations

University Museums: Many colleges have free entry to smaller but interesting exhibits.

Offbeat Museums: Quirky ones (like museums dedicated to neon signs or vintage toys) can be a fun change of pace.

Optional Extras

Self-Guided Tour: Grab a brochure or use your phone to learn about exhibits.

Snack Break: Bring your own water and a small snack if allowed.

Tips for Success

Kid-Friendly: Some museums have children's areas or interactive sections, so it can be a family outing.

Parking Costs: Factor in potential parking fees; look for public transit if that's cheaper.

Resource Recommendations

Museum Websites: They usually list free or reduced admission days.

Local Cultural Passes: Libraries sometimes lend passes for free museum entry.

08. Podcast & Walk

Why This Works

Combines a free audio entertainment source with light exercise and quality couple time.

How to Plan

1. Pick a Podcast: True crime, comedy, parenting, or self-improvement—something you both find interesting.

2. Walk a Short Route : Around your neighborhood or a nearby park.

3. Discuss: Pause the podcast at certain points to chat about what you've heard.

Real-Life Scenario

April and Zach listen to a 20-minute episode of a comedy podcast while strolling around their block. They often pause to laugh and share thoughts, turning it into a shared experience.

Variations

Indoor Option: If weather is bad, walk laps in a mall or do chores at home while listening on speaker.

Separate Earbuds: Each can use one earbud so you can still hear each other—and traffic.

Optional Extras

Post-Podcast Discussion: Sit on a bench or your porch to talk deeper about the episode's topic.

Different Genres: Alternate picks so each partner gets to explore new interests.

Tips for Success

Volume Control: Keep one ear open for safety if you're walking near roads.

Baby in Tow: Use a stroller or baby carrier if they're awake and calm enough to join.

Resource Recommendations

Podcast Apps: Spotify, Apple Podcasts, Google Podcasts.

Popular Couple-Focused Podcasts: "Marriage and Martinis," "One Extraordinary Marriage."

Conclusion

When finances are tight, ingenuity takes center stage. By rethinking everyday resources—from free local concerts to homemade pizza—you'll discover that romance thrives on laughter, conversation, and mutual support, not on lavish spending.

Chapter Seven

Self-Care as a Couple

Introduction

Parenthood is a transformative journey that can leave little room for self-care—let alone couple-care. Yet nurturing your emotional and mental well-being together is vital for a healthy partnership. This final chapter focuses on two date ideas geared toward reflection, growth, and recharging as a team.

01. Reflect and Recharge

Why This Works

Encourages open communication about what's working in your relationship, what's challenging, and how to support each other better.

How to Plan

1. Set a Calming Environment : Light a candle or sit in a cozy spot at home once the baby is asleep.

2. Structured Conversation: Use prompts or a "relationship check-in" guide. Topics can include gratitude, concerns, or future goals.

3. Listen Actively: Give each other undivided attention, acknowledging feelings without judgment.

Real-Life Scenario

Casey and Dawn schedule a monthly "us check-in." They ask each other three questions: "What went well this month?" "What was tough?" and "How can I support you better?" It keeps them on the same page emotionally.

Variations

Journaling Together: Write answers separately, then share.

Guided Workbook: Purchase or download a couples' reflection workbook for structured prompts.

Optional Extras

Relaxation Techniques: Start with deep breathing or a short meditation to set a calm tone.

Tea or Wine: Sip something soothing to make it feel more like a date.

Tips for Success

Stay Positive: Even if challenges surface, frame them constructively.

Time Boundaries: Aim for 30 minutes to an hour, so it doesn't feel overwhelming.

Resource Recommendations

Couples' Question Cards: "Our Moments" or "TableTopics" decks.

Relationship Books: "The Seven Principles for Making Marriage Work" by John Gottman for additional guidance.

02. Plan Your Dream Vacation

Why This Works

Inspires hope for the future, even if a big trip isn't feasible right now. Daydreaming together nurtures a sense of teamwork and excitement.

How to Plan

1. Choose a Format : Go digital with Pinterest boards or create a physical vision board.

2. Brainstorm Destinations: List places you'd love to visit—local, national, or international.

3. Discuss Activities: Beaches vs. mountains, city tours vs. nature hikes, romantic vs. adventurous.

Real-Life Scenario

Natasha and Philip have a "future travel map" pinned up, marking dream spots. Even though they're tied up with a newborn, they add to the map whenever they discover a new place, keeping the wanderlust alive.

Variations

Near-Term Mini Trip: Plan a small weekend getaway you can do sooner—like a short road trip.

Ultimate Bucket List: Include wild, far-flung destinations without worrying about practicality.

Optional Extras

Travel Shows or Vlogs: Watch YouTube channels on locations you're curious about.

Meal Theme: Cook a dish from a dream destination while you plan.

Tips for Success

Stay Flexible: Acknowledge your baby's age and changing needs. You might not travel immediately, but the dream fuels positivity.

Budget Talk: If you want to make it happen one day, consider saving strategies together.

Resource Recommendations

Travel Websites: Lonely Planet, TripAdvisor for destination ideas.

Vision Board Apps: Canva or Pinterest to organize images and notes.

Conclusion

Self-care as a couple involves consciously nurturing your emotional bond and looking forward to what the future holds. Whether you're sharing heartfelt reflections or daydreaming about bucket-list destinations, these moments of introspection and hope can carry you through the hectic days of early parenthood.

Conclusion

Raising a young child is simultaneously wonderful and challenging. Yet as you juggle diapers, feedings, and the million tasks of parenting, remember that your partnership deserves care, too. These 50 date ideas—ranging from quiet nights in to outdoor escapades—are tools to keep your relationship strong. Even when plans go awry (and they often will), the real magic is in making time for each other, again and again.

Afterword

Final Encouragement / Call to Action

Remember that your relationship forms the foundation of your growing family. Even small efforts to connect—sharing a 15-minute coffee break or dancing in the kitchen—can keep that foundation strong. Celebrate each other and the journey you're on together, knowing that every stage of parenthood brings new ways to bond and grow closer.

If you enjoyed these ideas, share your favorite date experiences on social media or leave a review to help other parents discover new ways to stay connected.

May these date ideas spark creativity, laughter, and deeper intimacy as you navigate life with a baby. Parenthood is a wild ride, but it's also a beautiful chapter in your love story—one that can be enriched by ongoing connection, adventure, and mutual support.

Enjoy your journey together!

About the Author

Razana Gober is a former world traveler turned devoted mom to two little ones under the age of two. With a background rich in adventure and exploration, Razana now embraces the beautiful chaos of motherhood while finding creative ways to stay connected with her husband.

This book was born out of her passion for keeping the magic alive in relationships, even amidst the demands of parenting and busy schedules. A collection of thoughtfully curated date night ideas, this guide serves as a roadmap for couples looking to nurture their connection—whether they're parents, professionals, or simply navigating life's many commitments.

Razana believes that being a mom is both the most challenging and rewarding job, and she's committed to showing that love and intentionality don't have to take a backseat to parenthood. Her hope is that this book inspires couples to carve out meaningful time together, creating a year's worth of magical moments that enrich their relationships and strengthen their families.

www.ingramcontent.com/pod-product-compliance
Lightning Source LLC
Chambersburg PA
CBHW070123030426
42335CB00016B/2251